Mixed Grill

A collection of poems for adults and children by:
Chrisi È. da Pavlova

– CHRISI È DA PAVLOVA –

FASTPRINT PUBLISHING
PETERBOROUGH, ENGLAND

MIXED GRILL

ISBN 978-184426-848-1

First published 2010 by

FASTPRINT PUBLISHING

Peterborough, England.

Printed in England by

www.printondemand-worldwide.com

CONTENTS

Poems for Adults

The Paper Boy

My Prayer

The Early Walk

The Lost Dog

The Trees

What a Life

Fairy Dream

The Stream

The Cat

Peaceful Night

English Weather

Wales

Poems for Children

In Praise of the Snowdon Range

Oh, speak to me of its beauty,
Untouched grey peaks rising heavenwards.
Pointing and jutting their heads always.
Grey, grey as the slate they stand
Looking forever stately and grand.
Firm? Well, 'tis not for me to say,
For pieces do come falling any day.
Large as houses they fall,
Nature unrelenting with her call.
Wild Wales, they call it, and aptly too,
Not many people or very much to do
If you are a town person.
But if like me, you are country bred,
Then there is magic with every step you tread.
A few patches of grass here and there,
Another part remains severe and bare.
The gushing waterfalls beneath Snowdon's peak,
Attract visitors every day of the week,
Pure and clear it rushes on;
To the Beris River itself, no doubt.
Many a pleasant healthy climb,
Is worth the effort, if you have the time.
Ascend a few hundred feet, and what can you see?

Why, the Snowdon Range from the Llanberis valley.
Standing there, unruffled, and dotted with trees,
Look across another way, and there is slate for use in the quarry.
Yes, a breath of magic grips you, secure.
You've been here before? You are not sure.
For only in your dreams do you think of this,
But to see it in its extremity is utter bliss.
On through the ages, untouched by human hand,
These mountains remain forever like sacred ground,
Beckoning, calling, inviting you there,
Willing you to climb them if you dare.

Lament for Nicholas

He is gone from us, alack and alas,
How we miss poor little Nicholas.
One minute he was there,
Smiling face, and fair hair.
Next minute under the wheels of a car,
Beginning his journey to afar.
He did not know what knocked him down.
Some stupid, rushing reckless clown
Who had no time. He only went for an ice-cream.
Pennies still clutched in his hand so clean.
The ambulance men looked very sad,
'I'm afraid he's hurt awful bad,
We'll see what the Doctors can do',
But sadly he did not last the night through.
His family all cried bitter tears of woe.
Why did the baby have to be taken so?
Young? He was only six
And just starting to mix
With all the children around here
Who held him very dear.
His Mother, who gave him all her love,
Saw her angel go back to heaven above,
To join his Father, and brothers too.
Silently on the wings of an angel he flew,

This little blond angel boy.
No longer do we see his toys,
Or hear his sweet, clear voice.
But it was not our choice
He was knocked down
By that stupid clown.
I hope his Mother knows, like I do,
God will love little Nicholas too.
One day she will meet him again,
Her heart-break will not be in vain.

Dedicated to a little boy knocked down in our street, 18th September 1972.

The Harassed Mother

'Don't do this children, don't do that,
Now come back here, pick up your hat.'
Oh dear, oh deary me,
Who would a Mother be?
'Don't we do anything right?'
Ask the children running for fright.

'Don't do this children, don't do that,
Now come back here, let out the cat.'
Paw marks everywhere I see,
Oh dear, more work for me.
I'll be glad when the day is sunny and bright,
Perhaps then things will turn out alright.

'Don't do this children, don't do that,
Now come back here, wipe your feet on the mat.'
The heavens opened up with rain,
And peace is lost again.
Back to school I pray they'll go soon,
Or else I'll spin myself a cocoon.

Untidy Daughters

'Tidy up your room,' I said to my two,
As I slipped and fell over a shoe,
One sock here, and one there,
I throw up my arms in despair.
A new blouse hanging on the end of the bed,
A new cardigan wrapped around Ted,
What things he must see as he sits there
So comfortably, in the old arm-chair.
Now, what's this I have found?
Why, it's Father's dressing-gown
Tucked underneath a blanket.

But there's more to find yet.
A drawing pin, a needle and a stone.
'I shouldn't be surprised to find a dog's bone!'
Just like little magpies they are,
Their bedroom has no bar.
'Can we have the animals up there?' they said,
'And tuck them up with us when we go to bed?'
Rabbits and guinea pigs? Oh, no.
That really is the final blow.

When will they tidy yet?
Not for a little while yet.

When boy-friends come knocking at the door,
Everything will be picked up from the floor.
Tidy girls they will be,
What a relief to me.

Praise Ye

Praise ye the Lord, ‘tis good to raise
Your hearts and voices in His praise.
His blessings flow, His mercies show
That He is good, to give us food,
Today, and every day.

Praise ye the Lord, ‘tis good to raise
Your hearts and voices in His praise.
His blessings flow, His mercies show
That He is near, you need not fear,
Today, or any day.

Praise ye the Lord, ‘tis good to raise
Yours hearts and voices in His praise.
His blessings flow, His mercies show
That He is mine,
Today, and every day.

Our Proud England

England once was regarded as great
But now it rests upon hands of fate.
Past leaders have come and gone,
Who helped to run the country and make it strong,
Famous names have gone down in history,
Shakespeare, Dickens, Barnardo and Harvey,
To name but a few
From the vast queue.
All did something for this land,
This green and pleasant England.

Women have played their part too;
Nightingale, Fry and Pankhurst,
Without them this country would have been all the worse.
We thank them in silent tribute.
The soldiers who fought for peace,
May their souls to freedom be released.

Famous names or not,
All have played a part in the plan
To make England grand.
Let us give them a big hand.
Now we are in nineteen seventy-four,

England needs to be grand as never before.
Her empire is growing smaller,
But she is still a solid, honest land.
Let all the folk unite,
Take up the eager fight,
England has been grand, and will be again.

To some of us, it is very plain,
We are trying to do our part,
But it needs us all to give our heart
And soul complete,
Then we shall inflation beat,
Strikes a thing of the past.
United we stand, united to the last,
'Raise your glasses, echo the toast,
England's our country, we give her our most.'

The Angel Gabriel

The Angel Gabriel was around last night,
Searching for the tiny light
That shone through the window pane.
But it was difficult because of the rain.
Quietly Gabriel flew about,
He'd find the house, no doubt,
There was a little child deep in pain
He had to take to the angels to reign.

Over the stars, sky and moon,
Not this house, not that one.
'This is it.' He'd heard the child cry.
Quietly, carefully, he looked through the glass,
The child cried, 'At last, at last.'
His arms outstretched towards heaven,
The poor one was not yet seven.

His chubby face all smiles now,
Gabriel tender, as only he knows how,
'Come, son,' he said, 'Come softly, do,'
Together through the sky they flew
On to that eternal land,
Where angels play in a joyous band.

The Orphan

"Won't somebody please let me in?"
Asked the little boy, ragged and thin.
The snow fell thick and fast,
The lad pondered over his past.
"Would it be opened if he knocked on the door?"
"Would the people inside be rich or poor?"
It was a small cottage, but friendly,
One of the smallest in Henley.
"Here goes," he thought, "They can only say 'No,
Boy, away you must quickly go.'"
Not everyone would welcome an orphan.
Many doors he'd knocked and
Been told to get off their land.
One more knock would do no harm,
If not, back to the old barn.

Bang! went the knocker sounding through the night.
He stood still, and crossed his fingers tight.
A little old lady came to the door.
She must have been about seventy-four.
"Come in laddie, come in do,
I'll find something for you,

Hot soup and chunks of bread,
And a nice, cosy bed."
In went the lad, gratefully too,
The snow had leaked through his shoe.
"I'll soon have you warm and fed."
A good meal, a cosy bed,
A happy ending for orphan Ned.

The Return

The throbbing engine of the great plane,
Is brought down to rest again.
Across thousands of miles it's flown,
Far off Africa was its home.
The great shining silver body lands,
As accurate as the schedule planned.
Who will be aboard, and sitting in the seats?
Why, 'tis someone we have come to meet.
Far from heat, natives, and dusty plain.
Back to England's grime and drizzly rain,
Come these departed folk.
Wanting to see us, we hope.

Temporarily forgotten are the black boys,
As we greet you with renewed joys.
No sitting in the sun drinking cola,
Might as well be in the Polar.
Summer here, as not begun,
'Have you taken all the sun?'
You're looking very fit and brown,
A drink will help emotion drown.
And then we will tales and progress relate,
Until again we are up to date.

Suzana

I have your photo before me, on the table,
And I try to visualise you, as best I'm able.
Creamy skin, and short dark hair,
How I wish that you could share
The things of the West.
I know you are fed the very best
That is possible. But don't you miss the fond embrace
That is the right of children of an affluent race?
Miss the soft touch of a Mother at night,
Tucking you up in bed?
What mysterious worlds lie across the sea
Separating us from you in their enormity.

So wistful you stand there
Holding your toy,
But gazing at your photo fills me with joy,
Your flowered trousers and your happy coat,
A warm jumper tucked up round your throat.
So you like music? We are happy to know
You bring from your violin
Thoughts from your deepest within.

With the vibrations, your body will glow,

You believe in our God too,
Our pretty little Sue,
Trust in Him, and don't wonder why
He made you a refugee.
We all have to play a part,
Cheer up, and please take heart,
I'm glad your name came to me.

My little jewel from the East,
I'll try and do as much as I can,
Because I love you, my little Suzana Han.

Dedicated to our refugee Korean daughter, early 1970s.

A Dying Wish

Write one poem every day,
Of the time that I'm away,
Said my love to me,
As we parted company.

Where he has gone, I cannot tell.
But I think it's heaven, not hell.
You always have heaps to say. So you'll have something for every day.
Tell them of the things we loved.
And of God who lives above.

How he was always on our side,
And came through life with us to abide.
Tell them of our children too,
The tricks they played on you.

How they filled my pipe with strips of wool.
And took the handles from the garden tools.
The picnics by the stream we often had,
Bought hours of pleasure, and made us glad.
The struggle and determined will,
When faced by an outsize bill.

The promotion at work that never came.

Although I went on trying just the same.
The worry and pain when you were ill,
It seemed as if my heart stood still.
Then all at once, our girl and boy,
Came home and told us of their joy.

Each had found their life's mate,
And wanted to get into a married state.
Time went on, what did we see?
Why? Children clustered round our knee.
Granny and Granddad they called us.
And of them we made an awful fuss.

Because we were so happy to be,
Together in each others company.
Suddenly his words were no longer clear.
This man who I held so wonderfully dear.
Every minute his strength was ebbing away.
He'd be on the other side by break of day.

In a last effort he said to me,
Your all that a wife could ever be,
Loving, loyal, firm as a rock,
To all our delightful flock.
Nothing more could any man ask,
As from this world he is about to pass

He said, 'Write it all down in a book',
Then anyone who likes may look,
And see what you have meant to me,
For more than half a century.
My dearest, my work on earth is done,
Someone else's has just begun.

Take my hand and hold it tight,
For in me there is no fight.
I'm at peace with God and man.

Seventy eight glorious happy years,
Occasionally misted by a tear.
But we had better now part,
Because of the strain of my heart.
So I kissed him, and stood away,
And saw him taken, that very gay,
Beloved, unequal, lover of mine,
Who made my life so very fine.

Blessed be the day we happened to meet.
For serving with him was a wonderful treat.
And now he's gone, I've memories good,
To give me each day my spiritual food. Soon
Ill be with you once again,
And end my broken-hearted pain.

Captain Joe

Tramp, tramp,
Go the soldiers' feet on the cobbled stones,
Marching to conflict.
Such a banging of drums,
And a tramping of feet,
The whole village is out in the street.
As they march, their heels smartly click,
To the battle they must go
And fight the foe.

Tramp, tramp,
On they go.
Bang, a gun is fired!
The man at the front of the army stops, dead,
For he is shot in the head.
They asked not for war,
But wishes cannot always be given.
That brave man, Captain Joe,
Is mourned, but not by his foe.

Tramp, tramp,
Nowadays everyone clusters round Grandfather's knee,
To hear the sad tale of Captain Joe,
Who lost his life in ages long ago.

The Absent Sausages

Which dish shall I serve my love tonight?
Sitting there with knife and fork held tight.
Sausages, eggs and chips?
No! They give me the pip.
Day after day, he would say,
'Serve sausages and you'll make my day.'
Pink, naked, funny shaped things,
I love poking them with pins.

'Sausages dear, tonight for tea?'
'No, it's like this you see.
Mrs Smith stopped me in the street,
Her grandchildren I had to meet.
The butcher had sold out when I got there,
His shop was scrubbed clean and bare...
Sorry, my dear, tonight it's fish.'
(I'll probably hear some comments about this).

'Mind the bones,' I said, as I placed the plate
In front of him. He began to state,
'Up early tomorrow my sausages to buy,
I'll not have you my favourite food deny.'

Tribute to Grandfather

Eighty-one and not out,
That's a grand old age, no doubt.
Happy birthday, Grandad, and many more,
Let's hope you reach five score.

What a strange world it will be then.
Nineteen eighty three,
What picture does that conjure up for me?
Holiday trips to the moon,
(Better book your ticket soon),
Electric this, electric that,
While we can laze and grow fat,
A robot putting in the seeds,
Another pulling out the weeds.

Let's look back to eighteen eighty three
What a different scene we see.
Steam trains pulling their load,
Less traffic on the road.
Green fields and flowering parks,
Ideal for walks in the dark.
Everyone moving at a steady pace,
Not joining in the eternal rat race.

But you've had an enjoyable life,

The love of a dear, sweet wife,
Two daughters and one son
Kept you amused with their fun.
The part you played in the war,
Like as many more.

Been very ill, but always pulled through,
Because God has work for you to do.
Friends, relatives, you have many
Who remember you every day.
So the best of everything to you today,
And may your smile long with us stay.

Born: 20.08.1883 – 30.03.1976

A Piece of Coal

I am a humble piece of coal.
Brought up from the earth's bowels,
Bad of shape, but black as black,
Soon I'll be put in a sack,
Go for a journey in a train,
Through the wild and pouring rain,
Put me with paper and wood,
Light us: and you soon feel good.
My warmth spreads through you well,
But to get hold of me is utter hell.
Men risk their lives to get at me,
Buried sometimes beneath the sea,
In all kinds of places I love to hide,
I'm not choosy where I abide.

When the train comes to a stop
You hear the familiar, clippety-clop,
Joe is there with his cart,
Ready for the rounds to start,
Up we go! I'm on top!
Going to be dropped off at the first stop,
It's Widow Brown's they decide for me,
She is just going to make tea.

'Come in, and have a cup,' she calls,

Old Joe says, ‘Thank ‘ee, Ma’am,
I’m real grateful, I am,’
Widow Brown says, ‘I’ll pile up the fire.’
Such a nice old lady she seems,
I feel cosy and start to beam,
Soon warm flames come around me,
While Widow Brown and Joe have tea.
Soon, soon, I shall be useless and dead,
But what a life I shall have led.

My Dream Baby

I dreamed I had a little girl,
As sweet as a new found pearl,
With soft pink skin and big brown eyes
That gaze at you with surprise.

She was lovely and cuddly and warm.
Although she had only a tiny form.
A pretty pink dress she wore,
And all eyes were turned when they saw
Her out in the street.

I married, and had my little girl,
As sweet as a new found pearl.
But one day she hurried to meet
A big dog, and did not see the car
Approaching from afar.

Now my little girl is not any more,
She sits with the angels up above.
And each night I send her my love,
'Cos I'll meet her one day, I'm sure.

The Countryside

As I wonder and ponder,
And sit over yonder,
I see hills and dales,
Mountains and vales:
With the eye can be seen
All nature is green.
It gives one a joy
With nothing to annoy,
How everything could be,
So beautiful to me.

Get out of my life!

I paid a visit to the Doc.
The time was ten on the clock.
'My chest is hurting me,
It's like this you see,
One side is fine, one is not:
Puts me in a difficult spot.'
'Take off your top,' the Doctor asked,
'Relate to me illnesses past.
Sorry, for an X-ray you must go. On it, the problem will show.'
X-ray not good news to me,
'You must have a mastectomy.'
Hospital very good to me,
'Would you like a clean nightie?
Pink or blue, which shall it be?'
I said, 'You choose for me.'
Ask daughter if dressings frighten her.
'Oh no,' she says, 'Does not bother me,
I've seen it all on TV!'
Have to visit Addenbrooke's.
Two gents take a look.
'We are going to do a tattoo.'
I ask, 'Who is Constable, who Picasso?'
One way to cope is cheerful front,
Alone, in private, the tears don't count,

Ride to Addenbrooke's it tough
But the staff for you can't do enough.
Two years on, I'm still here,
For that, I give a cheer.
Every ache, every little pain,
You ask has it come back again?
No, it's the arthritis, (half-righteous), a family joke
But it is not fun to poke
A laugh at illness like the big 'C'.
When dressed, nobody knows but me
What is under my clothes,
My (poached egg) is not on show!
A phrase keeps running through my head,
I do not wish to be dead,
I will survive.

Tribute to an Aunt

With loving thoughts of Auntie Lyd,
Who from earth's worries, she is rid.
To join other loved ones she has flown
Leaving us here alone.

In life she was gentle and kind,
With thoughts of others on her mind.
Her cheerful smile, the empty chair,
Her pot plants thriving with her care.

Everybody loved you here below,
We didn't want to let you go.
We hope you are looking at us remaining here,
And your spirit will guide us for many a year.

Mischief

A pair of hazel eyes, and a pair of blue,
Seeking, wondering what they can do.
A little twinkle, a knowing grin,
Watch out! The fun is about to begin.
Like fairies dashing about the place
They torment and excite the human race.

Two young girls, who would have thought
What mischief they have each other taught?
Shining eyes peep round the door,
You trip, and fall on the floor.
They did not mean to polish under the mat,
It was just unfortunate on the floor you sat.
With caution you proceed to a chair,
There can't be anything wrong here,
But there is! A slimy, muddy-coloured slug,
Cold shivers go down your back and you sigh,
'Ugh.'
'A nice cup of tea?' 'Yes, please.'
You relax now and feel more at ease.
Have they finished with you yet?
You can bet your life there's more to expect.

So the evening passes on
Until at last it's time for bed.

Good, you think, with a nod of the head.
When in bed and asleep they lie
Who would think they led you such a hue and cry?
Sleeping angels, hair spread out, eyes closed,
One look at them so calm and reposed,
But part with them, you have not the slightest intent,
Keeping up with them is time well spent.
Bless them, and let them sleep,
Until in the morning the sun begins to peep.

The Lonely Old Lady

I looked out of the window, what did I see?
Houses, washing, children, and a lonely oak tree.
Like me, that tree must have memories great,
I can't remember the exact date
We had workmen here with bricks,
And houses shot up very quick.
The washing hanging on the lines to dry,
Hearing the children let out a cry,
The lonely old oak tree is like me,
Many things he chanced to see.
As he stands on my land, tall and strong,
Like me, he's been here for many a day long.
We are old and changes come,
How the children enjoy the sun.
I must make friends with them soon,
In this beautiful month of June.

The Paper Boy

'Paper, paper, late night final'.
Hear the ragged boy call,
Standing shivering there
With trousers threadbare.
He is selling the news
And having chance to see our views,
Ever changing hour by hour.
The city gent with the flowers,
Taking them home for his wife, he said,
Who was at home, ill in bed.
The bent old grandma passing near,
Her smile fills you full of cheer,
The children playing in the street,
Muffled up to keep in the heat.
The poor old rag man's horse,
Treading his wearisome course,
He goes home to the field to graze.
And now the papers are all sold,
His pockets are not lined with gold.
But he has a home that is cosy and warm,
Where he can sleep until the dawn.

My Prayer

Dear Father, God in Heaven,
Wilt Thou be my friend,
Until life's end?
Help and guide me all the way,
Teach me to love Thee every day,
Show me how to do Thy will,
And to remember Thee when still?
To discourage from all wrong,
And sing unto Thee a joyous song,
And when at last
My sins are past
I'll dwell with Thee
In Eternity.

Amen.

The Early Walk

Over the dales and meadows gay,
Light-hearted, stepping on our way,
Cross one stile, ford a stream,
What a delightful place to dream
Of all the creatures of this earth
Who were put here to show their worth.
The horses grazing on the grass,
Just raise an eye as we pass.
Brer Rabbit shoots into a hole,
And a fox is seen, now a water vole
Is close by the banks of the stream,
Peering into waters of murky green.

A little further, what do we see?
Why, ‘tis a sparrow on a tree,
Chirruping a song so sweet,
To the ear it was a treat.
Fresh as the breeze that gently blows,
And the gentle stream that flows,
By the sides of meadow and dale,
Come wind, come rain, come snow, come hail,
Oh, the bliss of an early walk,
A good companion, lively talk,
Both are easy to obtain,

And what pleasure we can gain,
By sharing the miracles of nature,
With another of God's earthly creatures.

The Lost Dog

I let my little dog go for a run,
But when I called him, he would not come.
I hunted far and near,
My voice he did not hear.
I searched meadow and plain,
But 'twas all in vain.
We combed the streets riding a bike,
But of him there was no sight.
Perhaps he had not wandered far,
Was a comfortable thought spoken by Ma.

By the time the clock had struck eight
We gave up and closed the gate.
By chance a few minutes passed
And I looked, he was coming fast.
Over the gate he came,
My dog, just the same,
Head down, tail between legs,
How pleased I was to see,
He had returned home safe to me.

The Trees

Young trees, old trees,
What do I see?
Waving their arms to me.
Come, visit me if you dare,
Don't just look at me and stare.
Some of us are tall and strong,
Been here for many a year long.
Some are like newborn babes in arms,
We elders, protect them from harm.
The rest sink in the ground, firm and deep,
Helping us to steady keep.
Deep down, we are just like humans,
Protecting offspring while we can,
In the rustling of the leaves we speak,
Telling the saplings what to seek.
Put your roots down deep and true,
Whether you be an oak or yew,
Then you will be fit for whatever life brings,
Standing up tall and strong like a King.

What a Life

I read in a paper some time ago,
Puppies for sale: ten shillings each.
But it came to me as a blow,
When I saw the dog I wanted to teach.

He was a poor little scrap,
I had to use my scarf for a wrap.
So tiny and so fragile,
He could not walk a mile.

I took him home, and brought him up,
On bread and milk for his sup,
He soon grew to be large and strong,
And would run around the whole day long.

We trained him to be good,
And sit and beg for food.
He could be trusted too,
If asked by you.

Walks and a run,
He thinks great fun,
And when he's tired out,
You wouldn't know he's about.

So quiet he lays,
On the hot days,
So gentle he seems,
And yet he's mean.

Biscuits and bones,
He thinks he owns,
And would not dream to share,
Even when there's plenty there.

But I like him all the same,
Although he may not rise to fame.
He's still the same dear dog to me,
Wherever he may choose to be.

Fairy Dream

The other night, I had a dream,
I was eating strawberries and cream
Out of a silver dish, with a silver spoon,
While musicians played a sweet tune.
All around I could see,
Friends who used to know me,
Until I rescued the Fairy Princess,
When she cried out in distress,
From the great Dragon that came her way.
I stepped in, saved her, and made her day.
Upon my white horse I lifted her,
Then dug into my horse with a spur,
'Away, boy, to the Palace,' I cried,
Half an hour's riding, then I espied
The gleaming Palace, tall and grand,
The finest building in the land.
I asked the King for his daughter's hand,
'Sure,' he said, 'She's yours, is Princess Rosanne,'
And then I awoke, my dream was broken,
Mother calling to me, my eyes wide open.
Princess Rosanne I could not see,
She had slipped away from me.
Perhaps tonight, I thought, if I am good,
My Princess again I will meet in the wood.

The Stream

By the pretty little stream,
I love to sit and dream.
Little waves pass me by,
I sit there and sigh.
Cool as cool is the stream,
Tinted with shades of green.
Trees stand tall on the bank
And hold their arms down to the water.
Many years these trees have stood there,
Like soldiers lined up in ranks.
On warm summer days,
I love to sit and gaze
Beneath their cool shade
Until the sun begins to fade.

By the pretty little stream,
I love to sit and dream.
What famous person sat here?
Perhaps someone who lived quite near.
Maybe not, who knows, who will tell?
Not the trees, the secret with them forever lies.

The Cat

Oh cat, oh cat, of what do you dream?
Of silk cushions, salmon and ice-cream?
He lifted an elegant white paw,
And looked admiringly at his claw.
'I have no call to catch the mice,
The family look after me nice.'

Oh cat, oh cat, of what do you dream?
Of scraps of meat, and a dish of cream?
He lifted his paw in the air
And said, 'Some cats have never a care,
All food ready and a nice bed too,
For me it would be like heaven come true.
I have to go and earn my keep,
Not all day on silk cushions sleep.'

Some cats are born rich, some cats born poor,
But all are lovable to be sure.

Peaceful Night

Such a peaceful night,
Not a soul in sight,
Up above the moon shines bright,
In the distance a lonely owl hoots his goodnight.
Long shadows tread the path with you,
Which shortly will be covered with dew,
Onwards you go, enthralled with everything
And feeling you would like to sing.

Daytime and night-time are completely unalike,
See how beautiful the scene is tonight.
Trees tall and dark like soldiers in a row,
In the day, children rush to and fro,
In and out, and climb to the top
Of the trees. Now the little village shop,
Shutters buttoned down nice and tight,
Their cat not even in sight.
Possibly Puss has gone for a mouse,
'Cos there are plenty around the house.

On a bit further what do you see?
The peaceful stillness of the lea.
Stand there and breathe in the salty air,

And blue streaked fish here are not rare.
But wend your way home, you should.
All night you would stay if you could,
For what is pretty in daylight
Is far more beautiful at night.

English Weather

Wild the wind, but soft the grass,
We thought spring was here at last,
Cold winds a thing of the past.
Each day, a different kind of weather,
Is it rain? Do I need my umbrella?
No, today is going to be fine,
The sun is going to shine,
Said the man on TV,
We will have to wait and see.
Heating full on, extra woolly;
I would be thought a big bully
If the cat I put out in this.
He is singing, and his life is bliss.
Never mind, gardening will have to wait,
Everything will be planted, but a little late.

Wales

Beside the fast flowing waterfall,
Did you listen, and hear the fairies call?
Wales is known as the land of song,
The valleys echo with the refrain all day long.
What does it matter that England and Wales have been at war?
Many hundreds of years, have settled that score.
Wales is bare, and solemn and proud
Where grass has ceased to cloud
The earth. She has succulent valleys, and oh!
The colour of the greens, the trees, I love it so.
To look at it brings poetry to mind,
But to describe it hard to find
Enough words to do this land justice.
Dark and sombre the mountain peaks
Reach up to the sky above,
Patches of green, and grey and brown
Are watched over by God in his love.
A fragile bloom, here and there, struggling on for life,
Its roots clinging to the soil to seek
Nourishment from way down.
How green is the valley,

It's there for all to see.
Chunky white sheep there graze
And look at you in a daze
When you happen to pass them by.
And what of the miners, you ask with a sigh?
No, they are not forgotten. Digging deep into the earth's crust
For them, their work is a must.
Hungry mouth to feed, and grates to fill,
Over a hundred years, they do it still.
Yes: Wales is a land of contrasts, mining,
Farming, steelwork, weaving and singing,
And churches are dotted about by the score.
Sundays, the voices echo as never before.
To God they are giving their praises,
Each in his own way.
I'm proud to remember my claim to Wales,
(But through the ages the blood is a bit pale).
The honoured Hywel Dda was one of our kin,
So I've got a touch of Welsh blood, however thin!

Mr Rabbit

Our friends keep a rabbit,
And it has become a habit
Of ours to go and see
Him, when he is having his tea.
He screws his nose in greeting,
(Getting used to this strange meeting).

Oft humans come to watch him eat
His carrots, greens and wheat.
He lets you stroke his head,
Then he retires to bed.
'Erk, erk,' he grunts as a goodbye,
'See you tomorrow, but I don't know why.
These humans are a funny lot,
Would they like me to watch them eat hot-pot?
Of course not!
Still I must not grumble, I suppose!'
He says, and wrinkles up his nose.
'They love me, yes, they really do,
Look! They've left me a carrot to chew.'

Our Body

We have eyes and ears,
And hands and feet,
We use our hands to help us eat,
Our feet to walk the busy street,
Our eyes and ears to reason clear.
Each of us has a nose,
And feet have ten toes.
To help us walk, we wear shoes,
We use our nose to smell the food
To tell us if it is good.
We have two arms we can use for an alarm,
Two legs from which the feet suspend
Keep us balanced at the right end
When rushing to greet a friend.
White skin, yellow, black or brown,
Upon none of these pray frown,
God has given us each our hue,
To Him we owe our due,
And we are not to wonder why.

A Cat's Plea

Oh, little black pussy, there on the mat,
You are growing strong and fat
Because you eat all the fish
That I place in your dish.
Pussy says, 'I wish, I wish,
That you would fill my dish
Each day, with food fit for a King,
Then I would sing, and sing, and sing.
My friends to dinner I'd bring,
Because they live on odds and ends,
They have not got such a good friend
As I have in you, lady dear,
Please hear my voice, loud and clear.
My friends I will tell tonight,
Tomorrow at dinner we'll unite
To feast like furry Kings,
Then all afternoon to you we'll sing.'

The Simple Things

The simple things of life are best.
It does not matter how you are dressed
For a walk down by the sea,
To see the water clear and free,
Rush to and fro, to and fro.
The cows in the fields low,
Really they are saying, 'Hello'.
The birds above on the wing,
A happy song they sing.
The green grass beneath your feet,
And now a field of waving wheat,
To be made into bread to eat.
And the trees tall and dark
Stand guard over the park.
A squirrel rushes through the trees,
And throws some nuts: They hit your knees!
Lift up your head, what can you see?
All things are beautiful to me.
God has made the Nature world grand
Throughout this England.

Mr. Gnome and Unbelieving Mother

Once there was a little gnome,
Among the flowers he used to roam.
Each evening when the sun had set
And the dew upon the ground was wet,
He would come dressed in a green suit
And sit and play his flute.
Upon the rockery he perched,
Each evening for him we searched,
But it was in vain,
We searched again, and again.
His music was so sweet to hear,
Tinkly, and crystal clear.
Mother did not believe in gnomes.
'They do not visit people's homes,'
She said. 'They dance with fairies in the park,
When it is evening and dark.'
'We will make her believe us,' we said
That night, as we went to bed.
From the window we watched, and saw
A tiny bell, swinging, moving along,
No person, but a voice in gentle song:
Mr. Gnome had come as before.
He must have known about Mother,
(Perhaps told by our big brother).
Anyway he left behind the tiny bell,

In the morning we found it, though hidden well,
And showed it to Mother, who said, 'My, my,
Mr. Gnome really does come then?'

The Wheat

Waving golden in the sun,
The tall ears of wheat
Ready to make into bread to eat.
Large loaves or small,
Brown bread or white,
We will eat them everyone
Each day when the baker makes his call.

The Birds

I hear sweet birdsong every day,
As in my bed, I cosy lay.
'Tweet, tweet,' they sing in glad refrain,
'Tweet, tweet,' and 'Tweet' again,
Birdsong so sweet and clear
A delight to the human ear,
Saying how happy they are once more,
That summer has arrived like before,
They sing from morning till night,
(They started when it was just light).
Long may the summer days remain,
So we can hear the glad refrain,
'Tweet, tweet, tweet,'
So very sweet.

A Plea

Please help me to be good,
And trust folks as I should.
All are equal on this earth,
Love them for what they are worth.
Red, or white, yellow or brown,
It city grand or shanty town,
Let me to them kindness show,
The world a better place will grow.

Sing a song

Sing a song of love each day,
Have fun, be merry and gay.
Life on earth is much too short,
Before to Heaven you are caught
In the great network of plans.
For those left behind on land
Gabriel sits up there,
With trumpet loud and clear,
Peter marks the great book,
He has only to take a look
To see how you behaved here below,
It's in the pages, for all to know.
So sing a song of love,
To your Maker up above,
Then be ready to fly on the wings of a dove,
When your number from the book is called.

Nature, Man and War

The fat
Black cat
On the mat
Cosy sat.
Round his body his tail curled,
Not a care in the world.

The spaniel dog,
Round like a bacon hog,
Head resting on his paws,
Not a thought of wars.

Little bird in the tree
Sings a song to me,
The busy little ants
Scamper through the plants.

Only man cares about the mess we are in,
Nature carries on as before,
Has not time to stop for wars:
Man started wars, and man alone must win.

Stood Up

'Well, my wise one, my friend the cat,
What do you make of that?'
All ready with new dress and shoes
And now I've got the blues,
My friend he's taken out instead,
Up the garden I've been led.
So handsome, and so neat and clean,
So sincere he did seem.
But now he's proved it's no go
And taken Dora to the show.
Oh well, if he asks me out again
I'm going to make it very plain,
That I've someone who will not let me down,
And he does not live the other side of town.
He lives right here, with me:
My black cat, named Smokey.

Sambo

Sambo, Sambo, the Persian cat,
Who loves to sit on the mat.
A beautiful black coat he has,
And four little white paws,
A white chest, and a smudge on his nose,
No wonder he's the cat I chose.
So friendly and so comforting he is,
With him, life is complete bliss.
No mice around our run,
Sambo was there to see them come
From their hiding place in the shed,
When he went in there to bed,
Quickly and quietly he sprung,
Caught Mickey on the run,
Then Minnie came out too,
But what did Sambo do?
A quick box of the ears to each,
Now they've moved home out of his reach.

Fish World

Oh fish, oh little fish,
Swimming in the dish,
Don't you sometimes wish
To see the outside world
Instead of going round and round?
Come and see what life abounds
In the streams about this house.
First, away scampers a mouse,
Then a furry bank vole
Hurries to his hidey-hole.
A fat duck waddles along the bank,
Four goslings walk in rank
Behind their mother.
On the green sit two lovers.
Up above the sky is blue,
And reflects a beautiful hue
Into the clear stream.
Along swims a bream,
Now a shining trout,
Going to see about
His business. Other little fish swim on.

Watching, I want to break into song.
As the water ripples strong
Over the pebbles brown,

I long to just sit down
And watch the busy water green,
For all manner of things can be seen
Rushing to and fro: fishes, insects,
And anything else you can expect
To see if you closely watch
The water any time of day
Whether it be in April or May.

Pinky and Perky

Pinky and Perky they are called,
And when we had them, they were almost bald.
Two guinea pigs they are,
Come to us from afar.
Funny little things they seem,
But they thrive on the cream.
'Ick, ick', they often cry,
The food trough had run dry.
Such tubby animals, so much food,
They eat anything, and think it's good.
Bananas and buns we slip to them,
Pushed through the holes in the pen.
Quickly it's gone, they cry for more,
And hungrily begin to eat their straw.
Ten times a day we could their dishes refill,
But I'm sure they would cry still.

Snowy

The name he's called is Snowy,
A white rabbit you see.
Could you think of a better name?
No, you would suggest the same.
Long floppy ears, and big feet,
To see him is a treat.
So sad he was when we took him in,
Dull eyes, neglected, unhappy and thin;
A good dish of oats, and of milk,
His coat is now soft as silk,
His gentle eyes smile when they see
Us come up the path with his tea.
'Here is someone who loves me, I know,
And a strong rabbit I shall grow.'

Bobby the bunny

Bobby is a beautiful bunny,
But he cost a lot of money.
Getting him home was a game,
In a box on the bike he came.
A soft, greyish brown coat he has,
And brown alert eyes, and great big feet
That stamp on the cage when he wants to eat.
Of course he has his little fads,
Bananas, peanuts and toast
Are what he enjoys the most.
'Erk, erk,' he says in way of thanks,
Otherwise he would get a light spank.
Out for a walk he thinks a treat
Hopping round and round your feet,
Until at last he's weary and content,
Then back to his hutch he is sent.

Teddy Bear

Hallo, hallo there,
I'm a little teddy bear,
Covered in golden fur.
It makes me want to purr.
I'm as happy as can be,
I've been living with Anne's family
For a little while.
I like living with Anne.
My bed is the dolls' pram.
Soft blankets cover me at night,
Help me sleep very tight.
Live is very good to me,
Since Santa dropped me down the chimney.

Tinker

Tinker, Tinker, man's best friend,
My wages on him I spend.
Biscuits, bones, collar and a chain,
But what a friend I have gained.
Dog is man's best friend, they say,
Guarding him throughout the day,
Tinker has proved this to be true,
No unwelcome guests to our house drew
Up in their cars. 'Woof, woof,' so fierce he sounds,
Nobody ventures out of bounds.
If they chanced, Tinker would have them quick,
Before the lock they could pick.
Only a mongrel is my dog,
He leads me home in the fog.
Paws on lap, eyes gaze into my face,
Who'd put a dog in his place
Out there in the cold, grey snow
When the fire has a warming glow?
He's all a dog could ever be:
Trusting, faithful and a friend to me.

Peter the pup

Peter the pup,
Had nothing to sup,
So away he did roam,
Far from his home.
He stopped on his way,
At the meadow of hay,
Where he'd left bones before,
But no luck, on once more,
Then to his nose came aromas of food,
'Oh my, this smells good,'
Off went Peter on the trail,
To find the soup swinging in the pail.
It was gypsies camping there,
With torn clothes and feet bare.
'Go away, dog,' they cried,
When poor Peter they espied.
Peter trotted away from them sad,
What! Did they think him mad?
And then he came in sight
Of a cottage with a light.
'Woof, woof,' said Peter at the door,
'Be off,' said a man, 'I've room for no more.'
So off slinked Peter again,
And then it began to rain.
On and on he went,

And picked up another scent:
It was a tramp in a hut,
From the rain, trying to put up.
'Come in dog,' he greeted Pete,
'I'll find you something to eat.'
So in went Peter quite content,
His energy all spent.
His friend found him a bone,
And said, 'Why did you leave home?'
'Because they had nothing for me to eat,
So I had to take to the street.'
'You come and stay with me,'
Said the Tramp, 'And you will see,
That we will be pals and share
Everything we find, from meat to a pear.'

Blacky-black

Blacky-black is my name,
And I have a lovely game,
Tying up all the wools,
Pulling it from the balls.

Blacky-black is my name,
And I have a lovely game,
For when Mother goes to the shops,
I, on the bed, quickly hop.

Blacky-black is my name,
And I have a lovely game,
Muddling sheets and pillows, oh,
How all the feathers go!

Blacky-black is my name,
And I have an owner who loves me all the same,
For I am only a little kitten,
And her love to me she has given.

Next Door's Animals

Have you seen the big, black dog?
The one that lives next door?
The other day he fell in a bog
And was covered in mud, from head to paw.

Have you seen the ginger cat?
That one that lives next door?
The other day he caught a rat
As big as his paws all four.

They have a tame monkey,
These people next door.
The other day, a rainy day,
He smashed the china to the floor.

Have you seen the rabbit
The people have next door?
The other day he broke his hatchet
With one of his long claws.

Lastly, have you seen
These animals are always clean,
They are looked after by Joe and May,
And given fresh food every day.

Christmastime

Christmas is a time of cheer,
Plenty to eat, barrels of beer
To quench the thirst of the singers who
Sing carols that are ever new.
How deep the snow lays,
Still they sing their round-e-lays.
Bringing the message as old as time,
Jesus was born in a stable not fine.
Come to save you and me,
We would like him to see
All the things we have invented.
But people have not relented,
Still their wicked ways do chill,
The hearts of others who bear no ill.
Love your brothers, black and white,
Go and stop the wars tonight.
Peace on earth, good will to all,
Should the message from wall to wall.

Wild wind or ghost of Èmilie?

Wild moans the wind
Coming up behind
The little cottage. Standing there
Desolate and bare.
Only the wind to haunt it now,
No worried humans who beat their brow
Asking what is that noise?
Is it a sad voice from the past,
Released at last
Our peace to destroy?
Both ours and our boys,
A ghost of little Èmilie,
Come back us to see.
Poor little Èmilie, our baby dear,
Taken from us, just as we moved here.
No, 'tis the wind that whistles round
The cottage. Èmilie is below, in the ground,
Deep in a box, secure and sound.
Only the memories rebound.
Mr Wind, you can huff and puff,
This poor family have had enough.
Never will they return to the cottage small
You can puff, and puff, and have yourself a ball.

Come and Play

Come all you children young and gay,
Come into the fields to play.
We will have laughter and games all day,
Remember the winter, cold and grey?
Now the sun shines bright,
And brings a glow of delight.
Children playing cricket, how happy their faces,
Other children running races.
Everyone is bubbling over with fun,
From their day of playing in the sun.
When the sun goes down,
They watch the clown,
Who belongs to a circus
(I wonder if they would take us?)
They have a caravan of bright green
Which is kept spotlessly clean.
All the circus animals are very good,
Some sit up and beg for food,
Others take you for rides,
And sometimes you happen to slide,
But it is very good fun,
On a hot summer day.

My Black Cat

A large black cat,
Sat on the mat,
Misery on his face,
Because he was in disgrace.

That big black cat,
He sat and spat
When I was near,
But I had no fear.

The wicked old boy,
Is cunning and coy.
He stole a fish
From out of the dish.

That little fish
Was for my dinner.
That big cat!
The wicked sinner.

Never mind, Puss,
All forgiven
I'll give you a drink
That'll make you think.

I’m sorry I took the fish
From out of the dish,
But I’ll sing a song
To right the wrong.

A lovely song,
Deep and strong,
From my black cat,
Sitting on the mat.

Night

The sun is sinking in the West,
The evening stars do shine,
The birds seek their tiny nests,
And I must seek for mine.

And I must seek for mine,
For below the stars I sleep,
When the night is deep,
I must seek a recline.

I must seek a recline,
Though the night is here,
For I fear no shadows,
Only the future I fear.

Holiday

Two little girls, one sunny day,
Went far into the woods to play.
They had such fun as they did roam
Till black clouds came, then they ran home.

Advice to a Cat

'Oh, you dear little pussy cat,
Sitting there on the door mat,
Why are you not catching mice,
Instead of making your coat look nice?'
'I've had enough of mice in my time,
I want to make myself look fine,
I'm going out tonight:
Going to have a fight
With Ginger from next door.'
'Oh, you are, are you?
Well, mark my words, 'tis true,
He'll knock you flat on the floor.'
'Oh, shut up,' says Puss,
'Why bother and make all the fuss?'

So Pussy went on with his fight
In the cool, pale moonlight.
In the morning, when he came in,
He looked bedraggled and thin.
His coat was pulled from his back,
And what else? One of his teeth he lacked.
Pussy said, 'I'll never roam
Away from my home,
I've learnt my lesson.
I'll stay and catch the mice for you,
'Cos what you said, was all too true!'

Green Fields

Green the fields, and soft the grass,
What more could anyone ask?
An open lap so soft and free,
Inviting you to come and sit with me.
Here our worries we can pour,
While sitting on earth's green floor.
She will not tell a word,
That may have been heard.
Tenderly, you sit and pluck,
The frail green grass, and hope for luck.
Why, here is a clover, four leaved at that,
Are you not glad, you here sat?
A quiet half-hour with nature's best,
Does much to put your mind at rest.
So, if at any time you feel the need
To relax, I recommend you sit in a field,
With all the soft, sweet smelling grass,
Your cares will be a thing of the past.

ND - #0260 - 080726 - C0 - 197/132/8 - PB - 9781844268481 - Gloss Lamination